CODES, PUZZLES, AND CONUNDRUMS

Mental challenges for curious minds

SIMON CHESTERMAN

Author of the Raising Arcadia trilogy

Marshall Cavendish
Editions

Cover design by Benson Tan
Illustrations by Hasyim Isa

Published by Marshall Cavendish Editions
An imprint of Marshall Cavendish International

A member of the
Times Publishing Group

Other Marshall Cavendish Offices:
Marshall Cavendish Corporation. 99 White Plains Road, Tarrytown NY 10591-9001, USA • Marshall Cavendish International (Thailand) Co Ltd. 253 Asoke, 12th Flr, Sukhumvit 21 Road, Klongtoey Nua, Wattana, Bangkok 10110, Thailand • Marshall Cavendish (Malaysia) Sdn Bhd, Times Subang, Lot 46, Subang Hi-Tech Industrial Park, Batu Tiga, 40000 Shah Alam, Selangor Darul Ehsan, Malaysia.

Marshall Cavendish is a registered trademark of Times Publishing Limited

National Library Board, Singapore Cataloguing-in-Publication Data

Names: Chesterman, Simon
Title: Codes, puzzles, and conundrums : mental challenges for curious minds / Simon Chesterman.
Description: Singapore : Marshall Cavendish Editions, [2018]
Identifiers: OCN 1046082580 | 978-981-48-2809-3 (paperback)
Subjects: LCSH: Puzzles. | Ciphers. | Riddles.
Classification: DDC 793.73--dc23

Printed in Singapore

CODES, PUZZLES, AND CONUNDRUMS

CONTENTS

EDITOR'S NOTE

This book complements the *Raising Arcadia* trilogy — but does not assume that you have read it. Those three books tell the story of Arcadia Greentree, a precocious teenager who must use her intellect and her wits to unravel the mystery that has shrouded her since birth. The present volume draws on some of the intellectual challenges she confronts along the way, as well as entirely new problems — and a few that are very old indeed. It will be of interest to anyone who enjoys thinking, does not mind occasionally being stumped, and takes pleasure in an elegant solution.

INTRODUCTION

From an early age, my daughter Arcadia demonstrated some facility in deciphering codes, solving puzzles, and doing whatever it is that you do to a conundrum. My husband and I tried to encourage her interest in such endeavours by presenting a new challenge each Saturday morning. This book brings together some of the challenges we set for her, as well as some that she came across or devised herself. (Now that the exploits during her final years at the Priory School have gained her a certain notoriety, the publisher of this volume believes that there is a market for such a compilation. I have my doubts, but I suppose time will tell.)

The first part deals with codes and other such methods of obfuscation: hiding a message, sometimes as apparently random text or images, and sometimes in plain sight under the guise of an innocent (but irrelevant) surface missive. Arky and her brother, Magnus, would sometimes use these tricks to send secret notes to one another, but the use of codes in wartime and by modern spies oftentimes means the security of a communication is a matter of life and death.

The second part offers some puzzles and games that require you to use what my favourite fictional detective Hercule Poirot used to call the "little grey cells" in your head to find a solution.

These puzzles may appear to be trivial diversions, but underlying the solution there frequently lies a principle or idea of larger significance: that one should see a problem from different perspectives, that having a bad plan is better than no plan, and so on and so forth. I think Arky used to enjoy these the most because there was always a solution to be reached, even if the journey there might be somewhat tortuous.

The third part includes some conundrums: problems where sometimes it is unclear what the *question* is, let alone the answer. To be fully candid, I do not particularly care for these myself, perhaps because I usually haven't the foggiest idea how to proceed. Arky, on the other hand, still loves to grapple with the horns of such dilemmas. Now that she is at university, she tells me that this is somewhat like the manner in which she presently spends many of her days. I do hope the text conveys her enthusiasm more than my befuddlement.

The format of this book is — I must apologise in advance, and with no disrespect to the author — a trifle repetitive. Each part goes through several examples and shows how to approach or answer them. Some of these examples are drawn from my daughter's adventures, the publication of which has caused her no little embarrassment, but most are new. (Just as well, for otherwise this book would be quite a waste of your money.) At the end of each section is a little quiz so that one can test one's own skills. Although Arky tends to dismiss all such enterprises as "elementary", the present text thoughtfully categorises them as either "easy", "medium", or "head-scratching".

It is no simple task, I must confess, raising a child whose mind races far ahead of your own — on occasions racing far ahead, round the corner, and down a rabbit-hole. One useful method, I have found, is to keep that mind active. If, by chance, you are a parent with such a son or daughter, I highly recommend ripping out the pages with the answers (found towards the back of this volume) and hiding them in a safe place. When your son or daughter comes begging for an answer, or a validation of their own solution, you may then trade a correction or a confirmation for some useful task around the house: mopping the floor, raking the garden, and so on and so forth. These chores do not do themselves.

If, by contrast, you are one of those precocious children yourself, then do spare a thought for your parents. As someone once said, the job of a parent is to give children roots and wings: roots to ground them and provide stability; wings so that they can aspire to greatness. I suppose the idea is that a child's development necessarily involves a tension between where they come from and where they must go. (Those of us who actually *do* a bit of gardening realise that the metaphor is nonsense: is it meant to be some kind of plant-bird hybrid? Codswallop.)

In any case, I do hope you get some value from this book, but if not, please direct your complaints to the author and the publisher rather than myself.

Louisa Greentree

Post Script: I must beg your indulgence for a second idiosyncrasy of the text. It has been brought to my attention that, as the proofs of this volume were being edited, a contemporary of my daughter obtained access and inserted some of her own codes and messages. For the life of me, I cannot fathom why the publisher could not simply delete these emendations, but they insisted that something about typesetting and pagination and so on made it too expensive. Instead, they asked me to add this note. Which I have done.

PART 1
CODES

⌐C ‹E‹ L⌐⊡ ⌐O⌐⊃ ›⌐⌐V
‹E‹ ⌐⌐O ⌐O››⌐O⌐ LⱢEVO

For as long as people have been able to communicate, they have tried to devise ways to do so in secret. At least two thousand years ago, Julius Caesar is believed to have used a basic cipher that continues to bear his name. Such ciphers are distinct from true codes in that a *cipher* replaces letters while a *code* replaces words or other units of meaning.

1.1 CIPHERS

The most basic ciphers manipulate the letters in a message in a regular way that is reversible. Leonardo Da Vinci literally used so-called mirror writing to conceal text:

Can you decipher Leonardo's message?

(If you cannot, try holding the page up to a mirror.)

Similarly, a basic cipher is to reverse the letters in each word. Fi uoy od siht, ynam elpoep lliw ton eb elba ot daer eht egassem. Interestingly, if you merely jumble the letters but keep the first and last letters correct, text will still be legible to the average reader:

Eevn tohguh tehse ltetres wree jmubelbd,
tehy slitl mkae snese, dno't tehy?

One of the best known ciphers is Caesar's cipher. The Roman historian Suetonius recorded that Julius Caesar encrypted important messages by replacing each letter with the letter three steps before it in the alphabet.

Original	A	B	C	D	E	F	G	H	I	J	K	L	M
Code	X	Y	Z	A	B	C	D	E	F	G	H	I	J

To write the word "gem" using the cipher, simply replace each letter with the one three steps earlier. "G" becomes "D", "E" becomes "B", and "M" becomes "J". So the word "gem" would be written "dbj". (Note that the letter "Z" is treated as coming one before "A".)

So a phrase like "The gem is in the bag" would be written:

The gem is in the bag.
Qeb dbj fp fk qeb yxd.

Other simple substitution ciphers include replacing letters by their numerical place in the alphabet (a=1, b=2, etc):

3-1-14 21-15-21 18-5-1-4 20-8-9-19?

Such numerical codes can be made more complicated by adding a mathematical operation such as doubling the number.

The Freemason's cipher is another example of a relatively simple encryption technique that is simple to use but produces strange looking messages:

>⊓⌐∨ ⌐∨ ⌐
L⊏⊐⊐⊐ ⊐∪∨∨⌐⊓⊐

In all these examples, decrypting the ciphertext is made far simpler if you know the key. For Caesar's cipher, that means the number of letters to shift. In the case of the Freemason's cipher, it requires the recipient of the message to draw a simple diagram that serves as the key (and explains why it is also known as the pigpen cipher:

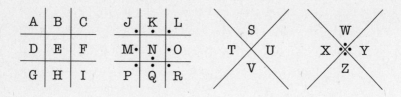

With enough text, however, it is usually possible to decrypt a simple substitution cipher without knowing the key. If you know that the message is in English, for example, it can be assumed to be made up of recognisable words. Computers now do such decryptions through brute force, testing every possibility to see what produces the largest number of words in its dictionary. But with a little imagination it may be possible to take some shortcuts.

Consider the following message:[1]

The code is based on one used in the Sherlock Holmes story "The Adventure of the Dancing Men". Without a key, Holmes is only able to decipher the messages using statistical methods after acquiring a significant amount of material. In the above message, if we add the information that it was addressed to a young lady named "Arcadia", things begin to become clearer. The third word has seven letters, the first, fourth, and seventh of which are the same. A reasonable assumption would be that that word is "Arcadia". Letters from that word are repeated elsewhere in the message. Substituting them in produces a plausible result:

1   *Raising Arcadia*, chapter 2.

ice d_e, Arcadia. ___ are _ear_ read_.

From here a little guesswork and some trial an error lead us to the translation:

Nicely done, Arcadia. You are nearly ready.

QUESTION 1.1: CIPHERS
DEGREE OF DIFFICULTY: MEDIUM

Can you decipher the following letter?

If you need a hint, remember that this is text in the form of a letter. How do letters normally begin and end?

If you need an extra hint, this letter comes from Arcadia's nemesis (mentioned in the blurb for "Being Arcadia").

Answer on page 88.

1.2 HIDDEN IN PLAIN SIGHT

Codes hide the meaning of a word or phrase. When the United States prepared to invade Panama in 1989, for example, the military operation was initially referred to as Operation "BLUE SPOON". The two word codename followed the Cold War practice of using randomly generated words for the purpose of increasing operational security. Just before it launched, however, the Commander-in-Chief of Special Operations Command complained about the codename. "Do you want your grandchildren to say you were in BLUE SPOON?" he is reported to have asked, incredulous. The operation was swiftly renamed Operation "JUST CAUSE".[2]

The most effective codes are the single use of a set phrase with a hidden meaning. Or it could be a symbol. During the American Revolution, two lanterns were prepared in a church outside Boston to warn of an attack. If the British Army marched towards the battle, a single lantern would be lit; if they crossed the waters in boats to a different staging ground, both lanterns would be ignited. "One if by land, two if by sea" remains a famous phrase in American history (and the name of an overpriced restaurant).

---

2   It is an oddity of the intelligence world that the most secure code words are typically written in ALL CAPITALS, meaning that they are the very words that leap out at you from the page.

During World War II, BBC radio broadcast "personal messages" into occupied France that were actually messages to the resistance — or red herrings to distract the Germans. A phrase like "Jean has a long moustache" had a secret meaning that only the recipients understood.

If used properly, such one-time codes can be impossible to break. The problem is that they require the hidden meaning to be agreed in advance. Complex codebooks that provide encrypted versions of many words can be created, but to be secure such books can only be used once each. Most modern encryption therefore relies on ciphers and the difficulty of complex mathematical operations necessary to decipher the information.

A less secure method relies not on disguising the words so much as hiding the existence of a secret message at all. A phrase like "The fat man walks alone" is likely to arouse suspicion, but consider a text message between two siblings that simply reads:

> Thanks for calling Arcadia, though I must say
> that it was nothing new. That's all 4 the moment.
> 'Bye now. Magnus[3]

This might be read as innocuous, but if you understood the significance of the number "4" and read every fourth word, you get a somewhat different message:

> Arcadia, say nothing 4 [for] now.

Another simple code is to hide a second message in each word after punctuation marks in the innocent text:

---

3   *Raising Arcadia*, chapter 6.

Arcadia, **do** let me know if you'll come up this
weekend, **watch** the boat races and stay for dinner?
Out of interest, **for** once you were right; **our** Mother
and Father did brag to me about your concert.
"**Parents**" as they say! **Magnus**.[4]

Slightly more complex are texts in which certain letters, typically
the first letter in each line, spell out a message. Known as acrostics,
these tend to be used more for poetry than cryptography. The
final lines of Lewis Carroll's *Through the Looking Glass*, for
example, are an acrostic that begins as follows:

A boat, beneath a sunny sky
Lingering onward dreamily
In an evening of July –
Children three that nestle near,
Eager eye and willing ear,

It goes on to spell out the full name of Alice Pleasance Liddell, to
whom the original *Alice in Wonderland* story was first told during
a boat trip.

More complex still are combinations of encryption methods
— ciphers that use code words and rely on prior knowledge
of the parties, for example. The following text hides a message
under multiple layers:[5]

Dear Arcadia, today's challenge will
exceed others. Real geniuses should
have no trouble with it. Code breaking
impresses no one: lies buried within
lies! In the end, the only thing that

---

4   *Raising Arcadia*, chapter 9.
5   *Raising Arcadia*, chapter 2.

anyone cares about is who won the war.
Second place is equal to last from the
standpoint of history. Column inches
shape that first draft of history as
we often see in great men and women's
rise and fall. Of course the days are
over when a trusted scribe could seek
to mould the way that your adventures
or reputation reached the public. This
highlights the way in which your every
deed lives on after your words and
especially punctuation. Message ends.

The solution combines two of the methods described earlier. As the text itself suggests, look at the words after punctuation marks. This produces: "Today's real code lies in the second column of this message." That in turn points to an acrostic in the second column of letters. Reading down those letters reveals: "Examine the ivories" — a reference to a piano.

Many other forms of code are possible. Some rely on hiding the true message completely — using invisible ink, for example, or microdots. The latter refers to text or images reduced to approximately one millimetre across — legible only under a microscope and able to be discussed as a full stop in a message. (Don't bother holding this page against a flame or under a microscope, however, as these are not practical methods for inclusion in a book such as this.)

QUESTION 1.2: HIDDEN IN PLAIN SIGHT
DEGREE OF DIFFICULTY: HEAD-SCRATCHING

Can you make out the message in the following text?

Once upon a time, 7AM
to be precise, 7 brutish
knights learned about one
princess who everyone said
had been taken prisoner by a
most fearsome monster. "Terrible
shrieks sound forth each sunrise,"
they opined, eagerly anticipating a
heroic duel pitting man against beast,
a daring prospect of love at first sight,
and also chances that a hefty reward might
follow. Yet on each knight's mind there
was troubling thoughts that the venture
could by various outcomes too gruesome
for imagining be their postscript.
They made it to her farm, rousing
a tremendous cackle from the
storeroom. "I fear you've awoken
the rooster," the girl declared. "Yet
the true quarry you hunt is
the first of each seventh. Toodle-oo!"

Answer on page 88.

PART 2
PUZZLES

Qebpb mrwwibp xob qll bxpv.
Xka exoaiv xkv lc qebj fkslisb qeb qeobxq
lc fkpqxkq abxqe fc vlr jxhb x jfpqxhb.

Ylofkd!

A puzzle usually refers to a problem or a game that has an answer or a solution. In this way it is distinct from a conundrum, in which there may be more than one answer — or no answer at all. Jigsaw puzzles can be put together, crossword puzzles can be filled in, and logic puzzles can yield a response that is correct and sometimes elegant.

As a warm-up, here are two relatively easy puzzles that might nonetheless take a little bit of figuring out. (Often, the "easy" part is clearer after you know the answer.)

First, a maths problem: a cricket bat and ball cost $100. The bat costs $99 more than the ball. How much does each item cost?

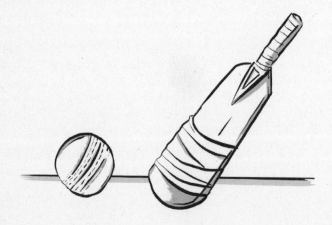

This deceptively simple problem causes many people at least a few moments of difficulty precisely because it looks so easy. Since the figures 99 and 100 are used, one might think that the ball costs $1 or the bat costs $99. Neither is correct. If you are still pondering, the answer is in this footnote.[1]

---

1   The ball costs 50c, the bat costs $99.50.

April

May

June

?

Another quick one, but no maths: Bartholomew's mother has four children. The eldest is called April, the second eldest is named May. The third child's name is June. What is the fourth child's name?

You might be tempted to see a pattern in the names and look for another month, or perhaps to throw your hands up and say that there is not enough information. But go back to the question and see if you might have missed something. (And if all else fails, the answer is in *this* footnote.[2])

---

2   The fourth child's name is Bartholomew.

2.1 MATCHSTICKS

Matchstick puzzles are as old as matches. When the short pieces of wood began to replace tinderboxes in the nineteenth century, a new form of entertainment developed around them. Companies began to print puzzles on the boxes in which they were sold and eventually books of the puzzles were printed in their own right.

Some are geometrical, with one or more shapes to be manipulated by moving a certain number of matchsticks. For example, the following is a stylised image of a giraffe:[3]

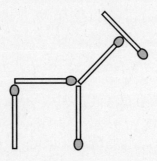

Is it possible to change the direction the giraffe is facing by moving only one match? It is, but requires changing your perspective on the direction in which the animal is facing:

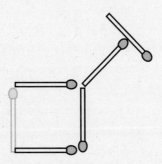

---

3   This is sometimes thought to look more like a donkey — though to be candid, it doesn't really look like either animal.

Another category of such puzzles derive from the fact that one can easily form Roman numerals using matchsticks. In this counting system, "I" is 1, "V" is 5, "X" is 10, "L" is 50, "C" is 100, "D" is 500, and "M" is 1,000. The numbers one to ten are thus:

1 – I
2 – II (i.e. one and one)
3 – III (i.e. one and one and one)
4 – IV (i.e. one less than five)[4]
5 – V
6 – VI (i.e. five and one)
7 – VII (you get the idea ...)
8 – VIII
9 – IX
10 – X

We can use matchsticks to represent a simple equation:[5]

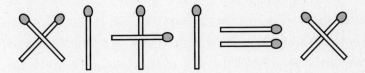

Which would read "eleven plus one equals ten". Eleven plus one obviously does *not* equal ten, so it is incorrect. But what is the smallest number of matchsticks that must be moved to make an equation that *is* correct?

One solution would be to add two extra matchsticks to the "X" on the right hand side, making the equation "eleven plus

---

4 Except on clocks. On many clocks that use Roman numerals, the number four is represented as "IIII". There are various theories as to why this started, but now it has become a tradition. A significant exception is London's Big Ben, which uses "IV".

5 *Raising Arcadia*, chapter 5.

one equals twelve". A better solution would be to take the first vertical match — the "I" from "XI" — to the other side and make X + I = XI. Or you could simply remove the vertical match from the plus sign, making XI – I = X.

But can you see a way to make a valid equation by moving … no matches at all? (Hint: try turning the page upside down and looking at the puzzle again.)

Another example uses slightly more complicated maths than addition. Again, the task is to transform it into a valid equation while moving the fewest matchsticks possible.[6]

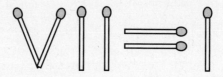

On this occasion, "seven equals one". Well, clearly it does not. So how can sense be made of this?

Straightening the two matches in the "V" and putting the next match horizontally would make II – I = I. That takes three moves. Moving only two matches, the V could be transformed into an X and one of the vertical matches shifted to the left, making I x I = I. Another possibility, moving only one match, is to take one of the vertical matches on the left and laying it across the equals sign to leave VI ≠ I. But that is hardly a "solution".

In this case, the solution requires us not to confine ourselves to Roman numerals but to consider other mathematical operators. Taking one of the vertical matches in "VII" and laying it across the top and to the right of the "V" makes it into a square root sign — and the equation reads $\sqrt{1} = 1$.

---

6   *Finding Arcadia*, chapter 7.

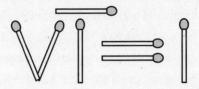

If you didn't like that one, you'll hate the next. Here the puzzle starts with a more complex equation:[7]

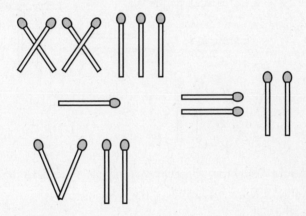

Twenty-three divided by seven equals two? Clearly not. (In fact it equals 3.285714 …, but Roman numerals are ill-equipped to handle decimals.)

Removing two of the vertical matches from XXIII would leave XXI; placing one of those on the right hand side transforms II to III — twenty-one divided by seven equals three, but there is a leftover match. Again, a single matchstick from either side could be placed over the equals sign, but making it an "inequation" is an unsatisfactory answer.

On this occasion, the solution requires a different form of ancient language: Greek. In mathematics, the Greek letter "π" or

7   *Being Arcadia*, chapter 8.

pi represents the ratio of a circle's circumference to its diameter. A well-known approximation of the value of π is $\frac{22}{7}$. By taking one of the vertical matches from "XXIII" and laying it across the top of the two matchsticks on the right hand side, one gets:

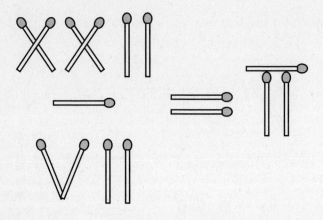

It should really be *approximately* equals, but 3.142857... is tolerably close to 3.141592..., the value of π.

QUESTION 2.1: MATCHSTICKS
DEGREE OF DIFFICULTY: EASY

Here's a classic matchstick puzzle to solve. There is a fly in this wineglass, but can you move two matches to leave the fly outside the glass?

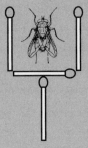

And a second that is more modern. Can you move three — exactly three — matchsticks from the shape below and leave exactly three squares?

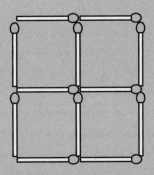

Answers on pages 88–89.

2.2 WATER, WATER, EVERYWHERE

Water is a theme in various puzzles — perhaps because, like matchsticks, it is an immediately understandable substance that is also able to be used to construct problems of varying difficulty.

Imagine, for example, six glasses in a row. The first three are full of water, the last three are empty. What is the minimum number of glasses you need to move in order to leave an alternating series of full and empty glasses?

An obvious solution is to move two glasses, swapping the second from the left with the second from the right. Or you could try to squeeze the two empty glasses from the right between pairs of glasses that are full. But there is a more elegant solution moving only one glass.

Pick up the second glass from the left and pour its contents into the second glass from the right. You have only moved one glass, and if you replace it in its original position it leaves the correct sequence of alternating full and empty glasses.

The fact that water can be poured is the basis of many other problems, with a classic type requiring you to use two or more measured quantities to make a third quantity. Given two jugs, for example, of five litres and three litres respectively, and an unlimited water supply, how would you measure out four litres?

Note that you cannot just estimate four-fifths of the larger jug — it has to be exact! The solution requires you to use the different capacities of the jugs and plan out a sequence of steps. First, fill the five-litre jug to the brim and then pour its contents into the three-litre jug. You have two litres left in the larger jug.

Discard the water in the smaller jug and pour in the two litres from the larger one. You now have two litres in the smaller jug and an empty larger jug. The important point is that you now have one litre of space left in the three-litre jug.

Fill up the larger jug once more and then fill up the rest of the three-litre jug. This will leave four litres in the larger jug.

More complex problems require more steps.

QUESTION 2.2: WATER, WATER, EVERYWHERE
DEGREE OF DIFFICULTY: MEDIUM

You are now given three jugs with capacity of eight litres, five litres, and three litres. In this case, the eight-litre jug is full at the beginning and you get no more water. Can you divide it in half so that two of the jugs have four litres each?

Answer on page 89.

2.3 CRY ME A RIVER

A different kind of water problem involves a river that is to be crossed with one or more constraints. Typically, there is some kind of boat or raft, which — for reasons that are never satisfactorily explained — can only hold a defined number of items.

The wolf, goat, and cabbage problem, for example, is more than a thousand years old. There are countless variations, but let us assume that a farmer has a wolf, a goat, and a cabbage that he must transport across a river. He has a small boat and (for some reason) can only take one item with him at a time. The problem is that if he leaves the goat alone with the cabbage, it will eat the cabbage; if he leaves the wolf alone with the goat, however, the goat will be eaten. How can he get them all across?

The first step is the simplest, because there is only one option: he must take the goat across. (If he takes the wolf, the goat eats the cabbage; if he takes the cabbage, the wolf eats the goat.) Then he leaves the goat on the other side and sails back. But what does he take next?

Actually, it doesn't matter. He can take either the wolf or the cabbage. What does matter is the following step: if he took the wolf, he can't leave it with the goat; if he took the cabbage, he can't leave that with the goat either. So he has to take the goat *back* to the original side of the river. He leaves it there and ferries whatever else is left (either the cabbage or the wolf), leaves the wolf and the cabbage on the far side of the river and returns to get the goat.

A total of seven crossings, really begging the question as to why he didn't get a bigger boat.

QUESTION 2.3: CRY ME A RIVER
DEGREE OF DIFFICULTY: MEDIUM

Another classic river-crossing problem involves three missionaries and three cannibals. (There are variations involving three lions and three wildebeest, but a wildebeest rowing a boat across the river is even less believable than a boat that can't carry both a cabbage and a goat at the same time. Another variation involves jealous husbands.)

So the three missionaries and the three cannibals need to cross the river. This time they have a raft that can hold at most two people and needs at least one to paddle it across. If the cannibals ever outnumber the missionaries, it's missionary for dinner — and that includes anyone in the boat when it is on that side of the river.

How can they all get across the river? (And no, no swimming allowed. Let's say the river is full of crocodiles and piranhas.)

Answer on page 90.

2.4 TO CHANGE A LIGHTBULB

Lightbulbs play an outsize role in thinking about intelligence. One of the most common ways to show someone having an idea is to conjure the image of a lightbulb being switched on. (It is tempting to think that humans must have been quite dim before the invention of the lightbulb, but then how did someone come up with the lightbulb, hmm?)

Lightbulbs can also form the basis of an interesting set of puzzles. One fairly well-known example involves three switches and an old fashioned lightbulb inside a closet, the door to which is closed. You know that one of the switches controls the lightbulb and that the light is currently off. The question is whether there is a way of identifying which switch controls the light if you are not allowed to touch the switches after opening the door. In other words, you can flick the switches any way you like, but once you open the door you cannot move them again. (And no, you cannot see light under the door, nor can you disassemble the switches to reveal the wiring.)

Clearly we cannot answer this with certainty if we can only turn the switches on and off. If we turn on only one switch, there is a one-in-three chance that you would identify it correctly. But puzzles like this typically have a more certain answer. It would make no sense to turn and leave on more than one switch. There is a one-in-three chance that the light remains off, in which case you know that it was the switch you did not touch. But again that is relying on luck rather than logic.

The solution requires a third option: not just on or off. Once again, the properties of the object we are considering become important. A lightbulb can be more than just on or off. If it was recently illuminated, it may be off but still *warm*. (Note that we were told that the light is presently off, meaning that it should be cool to the touch.)

The answer, then, is to turn on two of the switches — let's say, number one and number two — and wait a minute or two. Then turn off number two. Now open the closet. If the light is on, we know that switch number one controls it. If the light is off, but warm to the touch, it is controlled by switch number two. And if it is off and cold, it is connected to switch number three.[8]

---

8 Very well, let us also accept that it is also possible that the bulb has blown because of all the people flicking it on and off.

QUESTION 2.4: TO CHANGE A LIGHTBULB
DEGREE OF DIFFICULTY: MEDIUM

This puzzle requires a lot more lightbulbs. Imagine a long hallway with a hundred lightbulbs suspended from the ceiling. Each lightbulb has a chain that, when pulled, either switches the light on or switches it off. Now imagine a hundred people walking down the hallway. Each of these people has a number. Person number one walks down the corridor and pulls on every chain, meaning that every light is now illuminated. Person number two walks and pulls every second chain, meaning that those lights now switch off. Person number three pulls every third chain, and so on. At last person number one hundred walks down the corridor and pulls every hundredth chain — that is, she pulls only the last of the chains.

How many of the lightbulbs are illuminated after the hundredth person has walked the corridor?

Answer on page 90.

2.5 MURDER BY NUMBERS

Many puzzles are, at base, mathematical questions. It is not surprising that numbers themselves can offer good material for puzzles. Yet some of the more interesting puzzles give the appearance of being purely mathematical, when in fact the answer is quite different and requires a little creative thinking.

Take the following sequence of numbers. Your task is to identify the number that comes next:[9]

$$2, 4, 6, 30, 32, 34, 36, 40, 42, 44, 46,$$
$$50, 52, 54, 56, 60, 62, 64, 66, \underline{}$$

The sequence appears to be increasing, but not in a regular fashion. All of the numbers end in either two, four, six, or zero — though zero itself was not included. The series skips the teens and the twenties.

The very act of reading about the sequence may be taken as a hint that the numbers are not just numbers of things, but concepts in their own right capable of meaning — and capable of being written down. What do the numbers two, four, six, and thirty have in common that one, three, five, seven, eight, and so on do not?

Written like that, the answer may have become obvious: the series of numbers can all be written without the letter "e". Once that pattern has been worked out, we find the surprising conclusion that the next number in the sequence is … two thousand!

Another example also points to the need to think laterally about numbers. Take the following series:[10]

$$16, 06, 68, 88, \underline{}, 98$$

---

9 *Raising Arcadia*, chapter 5.
10 *Being Arcadia*, chapter 1.

What number fills in the space? On this occasion, the numbers do not entirely make sense. Sixteen then zero-six? Sixty-eight, eighty-eight, blank, ninety-eight.

As with an earlier matchstick problem, the answer requires us to look at the problem from a different perspective. Try looking at the sequence with the page turned upside down. Now the series looks quite different: 86, __, 88, 89, 90, 91. The missing number is 87, which may be written upside down as the letter "L" followed by the number 8.

QUESTION 2.5: MURDER BY NUMBERS
DEGREE OF DIFFICULTY: EASY

(a) *What number comes next in the sequence:*

    1, 4, 5, 6, 7, 9, 11, __

(b) *What comes next:*

    ST, ND, RD, TH, __

(c) *And finally, fill in the gap:*

    1,600,000, 28, 11, 6, 3, __

Answers on page 92.

2.6 CHE∫∫

Chess is a sufficiently complex game that it took decades for computers to be built that were powerful enough to beat the best human. For the first move, white has a choice of 20 possibilities: sixteen pawn moves and four knight moves. Then black has the same options, meaning that there are 400 possible board arrangements after just one move apiece. The numbers increase quickly. After two moves each, there are almost 9,000 possibilities; after four, that jumps to almost 200,000. After seven moves, it is over 10,000,000.

Whole libraries of books have been written on chess, many appealing to a niche audience of those whose passion for it is equal to or greater than their skill. Here, we limit ourselves to some puzzles that should at least be understandable — if not necessarily answerable — by anyone who is at least familiar with the rules of the game.[11]

We can start with a puzzle that is probably the easiest in this entire book. Imagine you are playing white in the game below. It is your move, and your challenge is to checkmate your opponent in no more than six moves.[12]

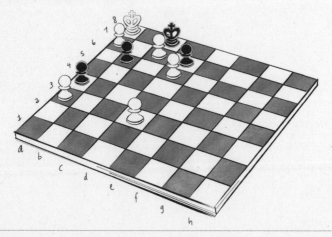

---

11 If you are not, either read up on them or else feel free to skip to the next section.
12 *Being Arcadia*, chapter 7.

Even if you are not skilled at chess, do not panic. One of the first questions you should ask in any chess-type problem is: what are the possible moves from which I can choose? Look carefully at the board above. How many legal moves are there?

One. Your king is pinned and all your pawns except one are blocked. All you can do is move the centre pawn. It is then black's turn, but all *she* can do is move her own pawn down the king's knight file.

For your next move, the same constraints mean that you can only move the same pawn, now coming to rest behind another white pawn and threatening stalemate. But black again has only one move, which is to move the black pawn down to where it is threatened by white.

Again there is a single legal move: to take the black pawn. Now both black and white has a passed pawn, each heading down an open file. Black will reach the end first, but the following move will see the white pawn checkmate black's king.

So congratulations! You solved the first chess puzzle — although it was, admittedly, impossible not to do so.

Most puzzles require a little more thought. Here we will limit ourselves to a category in which checkmate can be achieved in just one or two moves. First, a warm up exercise. White is to move and checkmate black immediately.

Do not be tempted by taking the black queen or sacrificing your own. If the white knight moves to e7, it checks the king, who cannot escape, block, or take the knight.

Many puzzles rely on knights, given their special movements and the fact that their attacks cannot be blocked. Others involve the promotion of pawns, sometimes in unexpected ways. Consider the following puzzle. Normally, when given the chance to promote a pawn, most players choose the queen as the most powerful piece on the board. But what would happen if you promoted the pawn to queen?

Stalemate! But it is possible to avoid a stalemate and achieve checkmate the next move. Instead of promoting the pawn to a queen, you should promote it to a *rook*. Then black has only one legal move: king to a6. And then white can swoop across to end the game.

QUESTION 2.6: CHESS
DEGREE OF DIFFICULTY: HEAD-SCRATCHING

Chess has sometimes been accused of driving people mad and this nineteenth century puzzle might lead some a step in that direction.

White has a clear advantage and it is her turn to move. But what is the fastest path to mate? Hint: the 1862 British Chess Association rules allowed for promotion of a pawn to any other piece.

Answer on page 92.

2.7 WHICH WIRE?

Pure logic puzzles can be presented in the abstract, but tend to be more interesting when given a bit of real world colour.

One could describe a problem, for example, as being the presence of three propositions — G, B, and R — and that only one of the following statements is correct: G is true, B is false, or G is false. It is a lot more interesting, however, to present the problem as a bomb about to go off unless you can work out which wire to cut.

So imagine, if you will, a bomb on which you can see three wires: green, blue, and red. A timer is counting down the seconds and you hold a pair of scissors with which you can cut one of the wires. The good news is that the bomb-maker has left you a note; the bad news is that it is far from clear what it means:[13]

Cutting one of the wires — one and only one of them — may stop the timer. I promise that this much is true. Next I can assure you that one and only one of the following statements is true: green when cut will stop the timer; snipping the blue will not stop the timer; or it might be that green when cut will not stop the timer. Onward now — never say die!

M.

---

13 *Finding Arcadia*, chapter 1.

So which wire would you cut? There are three possibilities: green, blue, and red. You also have three statements, only one of which is true: (i) green stops the bomb, (ii) blue does not stop the bomb; (iii) green does *not* stop the bomb.

The first and third cannot both be true: green cannot stop and not stop the bomb. And what about red? What happens if you cut the red wire?

To answer a problem like this, it helps to be systematic. There are only three statements, so you can test each in turn.

If the first statement is true, that green stops the bomb, then it is false that green does *not* stop the bomb, so (iii) is false. But the second statement, that blue does not stop the bomb, would also be true. Two statements are true so that cannot be the answer.

If the second statement is true, then blue does not stop the bomb. So it could be red or green. But just as (i) and (iii) cannot both be true, they also cannot both be false. If (i) is false, then green does not stop the bomb — but if (iii) is false, then green *does* stop the bomb. Contradiction again, so that cannot be the answer.

If the *third* statement is true, then green does not stop the timer. So blue or red. But the other two statements must be false. If the first statement is false, then green does not stop the bomb. So far, so good. And if the second statement is false, then ... blue will stop the bomb and there is no contradiction.

If we go back to the more abstract formulation, the three statements were (i) G is true, (ii) B is false, or (iii) G is false. If only one of these statements can be true, it may now be clearer that this is only possible if that statement is (iii), with the result that we know G is false and B is therefore true. (But it does seem a little more interesting when the stakes are raised and a bomb is ticking down ...)

QUESTION 2.7: WHICH WIRE?
DEGREE OF DIFFICULTY: MEDIUM

*This is a classic logic puzzle dressed up to appeal to a more
modern audience. Imagine a nuclear bomb is counting down
towards detonation. There is no chance of escape — your
only means of survival is to disarm it. Two wires connect the
detonator to its power source: one purple, one brown. Cutting
the right wire will disarm it, cutting the wrong wire will cause
it to blow up immediately.*

*You have with you the two women who designed the bomb
and who both know which wire to cut. They are identical
twins in every respect except for this: one of them always tells
the truth, while the other always lies. You do not know which
is which.*

*You may ask one question of one of the twins, the answer to
which must be either "yes" or "no". After you get the answer,
you must cut one of the wires. What do you ask?*

Answer on page 93.

2.8 FIRE!

Some logic puzzles are like riddles, requiring a counterintuitive step to solve them. Take the problem of the young woman trapped on a burning island.[14]

Forest covers this island. On a day when a strong east wind was blowing, lightning struck the easternmost point of the island and started the fire. The flames devour everything in their path, fanned by the breeze and moving from east to west. The woman's island is two kilometres across; in two hours, the entire island will be consumed and her with it. The only beach is on the eastern tip and impossible to reach. The rest of the coast is cliffs and jagged rocks, so she cannot jump into the water, either.

How can she survive?

Our instincts tell us that she should flee the fire, and that much is correct. But if she merely runs from the flames then they will consume her. There is another possibility, however.

She should start her own fire. Use matches if she has them, or else take a branch to the edge of the current blaze and light it. Then run with that branch to the western side of the island. The wind will keep the new fire moving west, so if she can burn the trees on that side, once that fire is out she can shelter there when the original fire approaches.

---

14 *Being Arcadia*, chapter 1.

QUESTION 2.8: FIRE!
DEGREE OF DIFFICULTY: MEDIUM

You have a lighter and two pieces of string. Each piece of string will burn for exactly four minutes, but it may not burn evenly. It may, for example, take three minutes and fifty seconds for the first ten centimetres to burn and then ten seconds for the rest.

How do you measure three minutes?

Answer on page 94.

2.9 WALK A MILE IN SOMEONE ELSE'S HAT

Some puzzles depend as much on perspective as they do on reason. The ability to understand something from another person's point of view may be central to emotional intelligence, but it can also help solve logic problems as well.

Take, for example, the story of an Arab sheikh who wanted to decide which of his two sons should inherit his fortune. The sheikh presents the boys with an unusual challenge: they are to race their camels to a distant city, but the one whose camel gets there *last* wins.[15]

The two lads wander about on their camels for days, approaching then retreating from the city. Neither wants to lose their inheritance by arriving first. At last, they chance upon a wise man and decide to ask him for guidance. Upon hearing his advice, they jump on the camels and race to the city as fast as they can.

Now, what did the wise man say to them?

He said: "Switch camels."

That is a relatively simple example, arguably more of a trick question than a logic puzzle. For a more complex example, imagine three people: Anna, Brandon, and Charlie standing in a police line-up and accused of a crime. Anna is looking at Brandon, while Brandon is looking at Charlie. Anna, we know, is guilty. Charlie, on the other hand, is innocent. The question is whether someone who is guilty is looking at someone who is innocent.[16]

At first blush, it might seem as though we do not have enough information to answer the question, as we do not know whether Brandon is guilty or innocent. But if we can assume that

---

15 *Being Arcadia*, chapter 8.
16 *Being Arcadia*, chapter 1.

Brandon must be *either* guilty *or* innocent, the answer should present itself: if he is guilty, then he is looking at Charlie (whom we know to be innocent). If he is innocent, on the other hand, we know that the guilty Anna is looking at him. Either way, the answer is "yes".

More complicated still are a class of puzzles often presented as being about men wearing different coloured hats, sometimes in prison. We can be a little more creative in the setting, though the underlying logic remains the same.

Four students of logic are captured by pirates and told they will be fed to the sharks unless they win a game that the pirates call "If-the-hat-fits". One student, Albert, is placed inside a large barrel so that he can hear what is going on but cannot see the others or be seen himself. The second, third, and fourth — Beatrice, Chandra, and Diaan-yi — are lined up facing towards the bow of the ship with Beatrice at the front, Chandra in the middle, and Diaan-yi at the back. Then the pirates show four hats to the students, two black and two white, and put one on each of the four captives in such a way that they cannot see the colour of their own hat. Chandra can, however, see Beatrice, while Diaan-yi can see both Beatrice and Chandra.

To avoid becoming shark bait, one of them must call out the colour of their own hat. If they get it right, all will go free. If they are wrong, all will die. All of them are completely rational and know that their fellow students are also. Who will call out, and why is he or she certain of the hat on his or her head?

To solve the puzzle, you must put yourself in the position of each of the students. Clearly, Albert is not going to be able to work out the colour of his hat, so he will remain silent. Similarly, Beatrice has no information about the other students, so she will remain silent also.

We are left with Chandra and Diaan-yi. Now, Diaan-yi can see two hats, one white and one black. She still does not know what colour her own hat is, however. So she must remain silent. That silence, nonetheless, speaks volumes for Chandra. Because Chandra can see a black hat in front of himself, while also knowing that Diaan-yi can see that hat and his own. If his were also black, then Diaan-yi would know that she was white and she would call that out. The fact that she does *not* do so means that his hat must be white.

So Chandra calls out that his hat is white and the logic students live to solve another puzzle.

QUESTION 2.9: WALK A MILE IN SOMEONE ELSE'S SHOES
DEGREE OF DIFFICULTY: MEDIUM

Albert, Beatrice, Chandra, and Diaan-yi's freedom does not last long. They are soon captured by a rival pirate gang and forced to play a new game (except for Albert, who is put in another barrel and does not play). In the new game, three students stand in a triangle facing each other and either a gold crown or a silver crown is placed on their head. The first to guess correctly the colour of their crown wins.

The pirates then tell them to raise their hand if they see a gold crown on another captive. All three raise their hands.

After a minute of silence, Diaan-yi calls out "Gold!" and wins.

How did she do it, and what crown are they each wearing?

Answer on page 94.

2.10 IMPOSSIBLE PUZZLES

If a puzzle is impossible to solve, it is not a very good puzzle. But there is a class of somewhat tricky puzzles that *look* like they are impossible to solve because there is insufficient information. The trick, then, is to find additional information in creative ways.

Take, for example, another bomb-defusing problem. On this occasion, deactivating the bomb requires that you enter the correct answer into a phone. At first, however, it does not look like you have enough information to do so.[17]

Here we are again! This time the stakes are a little higher, as there is enough C-4 here to bring down most of the building. There's just time to tell you a story. I call it "Fun with Dick and Jane and a Bomb".

M has planted a bomb that will detonate at one and only one of the following times:
2:00pm, 2:30pm
3:10pm, 3:30pm, 3:40pm
4:20pm, 4:50pm
5:00pm, 5:10pm, 5:20pm

M shows this list to Dick and Jane. She then whispers to Dick the <u>hour</u> at which the bomb will detonate, and quietly tells Jane the <u>minute</u> at which it will detonate.

Dick says: "Boo! I don't know when the bomb will detonate — but at least I know that Jane doesn't know either."

Then Jane shouts: "Eureka! I didn't know when the bomb would detonate, but I do now."

---

17   *Finding Arcadia*, chapter 7.

And Dick cries out: "Aha! Now I also know
when the bomb will detonate."

Enter the three digits of the correct time
into the phone and press "send". Congratulations:
you have disarmed the bomb! (Enter anything
else and, well, oops!)

Cheerio,
M

We have a group of possible answers. In such situations, there are two ways to solve the puzzle: choose the right answer, or eliminate all the wrong answers in the hope that only one is left. To do that, we draw on the limited information about what they know, what they don't know, but also — most importantly — what they know that the other person *does not know*.

Dick knows only the hour at which the bomb goes off; Jane knows only the minute. He doesn't know the time. But for him to be certain that Jane *cannot* know, then the time must not be one of the possibilities with a unique number of minutes — because if Jane knew that the number of minutes was forty, she would also know that the time had to be 3:40pm; if the number of minutes was fifty, it would be 4:50pm. For Dick to be certain that this is impossible, to exclude them completely, the hour cannot be three or four.

Eliminating the hour being three or four leaves five possible answers:

2:00pm, 2:30pm
5:00pm, 5:10pm, 5:20pm

Jane knows the number of minutes. If she can now work out the answer — "I didn't know then, but I do now" — then that number cannot be zero or she still would not know whether it was 2pm or 5pm. So those two times can also be ruled out, leaving three possibilities:

2:30pm

5:10pm, 5:20pm

"Aha!" Dick cries. Why? Because he can now work out the time. He has known the hour all along, so assuming he has reached a similar conclusion, then for him to know the answer it must be the hour with only one possible answer: 2:30pm.

QUESTION 2.10: IMPOSSIBLE PUZZLES
DEGREE OF DIFFICULTY: HEAD-SCRATCHING

This puzzle gained global notoriety when it circulated on social media described as being from a Singapore primary school test. In fact, it came from the Singapore and Asian Schools Math Olympiad, aimed at the very brightest secondary school students.

Here is the question in its entirety:

"Albert and Bernard just become friends with Cheryl, and they want to know when her birthday is. Cheryl gives them a list of 10 possible dates:

May 15, May 16, May 19
June 17, June 18
July 14, July 16
August 14, August 15, August 17

Cheryl then tells Albert and Bernard separately the month and the day of her birthday respectively.

Albert: 'I don't know when Cheryl's birthday is, but I know that Bernard doesn't know too.'

Bernard: 'At first I don't know when Cheryl's birthday is, but I know now.'

Albert: 'Then I also know when Cheryl's birthday is.'

So when is Cheryl's birthday?"

Answer on page 95.

2.11 LOGICAL PIRATES

Another staple of puzzles is the use of coins. Sometimes they are to be moved into patterns, reminiscent of the matchsticks with which we began this chapter. On other occasions, the task is to divide them, a point to which we will return shortly. But as a starting point, one may want to ensure that all the coins are, in fact, genuine.

Imagine, then, a pirate who is in possession of nine gold coins, one of which is counterfeit. He knows that the counterfeit coin is lighter than the gold coins and has a pair of scales with which to weigh any number of coins. (Such scales only show which side is heavier, they do not tell you the mass of a coin.) What is the minimum number of weighings you need to determine with certainty the counterfeit?

Clearly you could weigh pairs of coins in sequence. You might get lucky and find the lighter coin on your first attempt, but it could take you up to five efforts to confirm which coin was the fake. Is there a faster way? As in some of the earlier puzzles, the trick is to get more information as efficiently as possible. In this case, each weighing tells us something about what is on the scales, but it is also possible to have a weighing tell us something useful about what is not on the scales.

To solve the problem most efficiently, start by dividing the coins into three piles of three. Let's call them 123, 456, and 789. Then weigh two of the sets of three — 123 and 456, say — on the scales. The possible outcomes are as follows:

(a) 123 is lighter, meaning the fake is one of those;
(b) 456 is lighter, meaning one of them is the counterfeit; or
(c) 123 and 456 weigh the same, and the lighter coin is in the group 789.

So after one weighing, we have narrowed it down to one of three coins. As we do not know which of the piles it was, let us now call them A, B, and C. Putting one on each side of the scales will, once again, either show us the counterfeit or reveal that they are the same weight and that the fake is the one left aside.

For nine coins, then, we can determine in only two weighings which is the lighter coin.

QUESTION 2.11: LOGICAL PIRATES
DEGREE OF DIFFICULTY: HEAD-SCRATCHING

A group of seven pirates has 100 gold coins, which are to be distributed among themselves according to what we are told are "pirate rules".

These rules are as follows:

1. *The most senior pirate gets to propose the division. All of the pirates get to vote on the division, including the senior pirate who proposed it. If half or more vote in favour, they divide the coins in that way. If less than half vote in favour, the most senior pirate is fed to the sharks and they start all over again with the next most senior pirate.*

2. *The pirates are all perfectly logical and utterly ruthless, each seeking to get the most gold possible.*

3. *You are the most senior pirate and, all things considered, would prefer not to be fed to the sharks. But you would also like to keep as much of the gold as you can. What division should you propose?*

Answer on page 96.

PART 3
CONUNDRUMS

>ΠΓV ΓV ƎΕΓO ΓΓЦO Γ>

7ΓΕЦLOƎV >ΠJ> ΠJΛO
JOVVOΓV JΓO VΕ ЦΕΓΓO7

ЦΓΓO7 ΕO >ΠO 7ΓΕЦLOƎV
VΓ>ΠΕ<> ΠKOVΓΕOV

It is sometimes said that a sign that a child is becoming an adult is when he or she starts asking questions that have answers. The implication is that children maintain an innocence that allows them to ponder over — and interrogate their parents with — problems that may be impossible to solve, or even to understand.

Do trees feel pain? What is the difference between a stone and a rock? If a dog has a headache, does it know that it has a headache? Why? (Or why not?)

Appropriately enough, the origins of the word "conundrum" are unknown. First used by an English pamphleteer in the late sixteenth century, it appears to have been a term of abuse for a crank or a pedant. (Again, perhaps, appropriately enough.) Here, we adopt its modern usage as a problem that is difficult or impossible to solve.

Unlike the puzzles earlier in this volume, the problems that follow have no certain solution. Often there will be answers that are better or worse; but in some cases, the aim is not to get the right answer but the least bad one.

You have been warned.

3.1 TROLLEYOLOGY

One of the better known conundrums is the trolley problem.[1]

Imagine a runaway trolley — a kind of single-carriage train, heading towards a junction on the tracks. Its brakes have failed and it cannot stop. If nothing happens, the trolley will continue on the main line. Unfortunately, some villain has tied five people down to the tracks. There is no way to free them; no way to stop the trolley. If the trolley follows its current path all five will be killed.

---

1   *Raising Arcadia*, chapter 4.

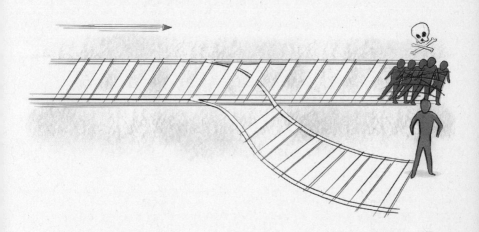

But there is an alternative. You are standing by the tracks next to a lever that can divert the trolley onto a siding. If you pull the lever, the trolley will move onto that track and the five will be saved. Unfortunately, that track passes through a narrow gorge in which a deaf workman is doing some repairs. There is no way to warn him or stop the trolley. So if you do divert it, he will certainly be killed.

So the question is: do you pull the lever or not?

The purpose of a dilemma like this is to strip a problem down to a fundamental moral question. In the hypothetical situation, there is no way to stop the trolley, warn the people, or come up with a third alternative. The purpose is, therefore, to see where our moral intuition lies.

In surveys along these lines, most people when pressed for a decision say that they would pull the lever. This appears to reflect a basic human desire to minimize suffering and maximize happiness: an approach to the world known as "utilitarianism".

But not everyone would do so. A significant number of people focus not just on the consequences of the action, but on the action itself. In this case, pulling the lever amounts to an act that ends the life of an innocent person and that cannot be right even if it saves five lives. This is termed "deontology", or duty-based ethics.

Neither response is right or wrong in the same way that a mathematical problem has one and only one answer. Here, the different answers reflect different worldviews. Does one focus on doing the right thing, even if the consequences are catastrophic? Or do the ends sometimes justify the means?

What is interesting is that, for many people, the way in which they view the world depends on where they stand. Imagine, now, the same scenario, though instead of a lever operating a set of points you find yourself standing on a bridge under which the trolley is about to pass on its way to the five victims. You know for a fact that a heavy weight dropped in front of the trolley would stop it. As it happens, on the bridge next to you stands a fat man of precisely that weight — and he is leaning against a weak handrail to watch the progress of the trolley.

Would you push him over the edge?

Again, we sharpen the dilemma by stating that you cannot jump onto the trolley and stop it yourself. Nor can you sacrifice yourself and stop the trolley, because you lack the requisite mass. Your only choice is to push the fat man or allow the trolley to continue on its path. So would you push the fat man over the edge to stop the trolley and save the five victims?

For most people, the idea of physically pushing another human being into harm's way is different from pulling a lever. Even though the numbers are the same — five lives versus one — the injunction not to kill seems to have more weight when considering a flesh-and-blood person rather than a switch.

Such questions are not entirely hypothetical. With the advent of autonomous vehicles, it would be entirely possible to programme a driverless car to prepare for various scenarios. MIT has set up a "Moral Machine" that offers dozens of scenarios that might confront driverless cars. Should two passengers be sacrificed if it would save five pedestrians? Does it matter if the pedestrians were jaywalking? If they were criminals? The results are diverse and fascinating. But if humans cannot agree on what to do, how are we meant to advise the machines?

Three quarters of a century ago, science fiction writer Isaac Asimov imagined a future in which robots have become an integral part of daily life. In this fictional world, a safety device is built into them in the form of the three laws of robotics, said to be quoted from the *Handbook of Robotics* (56th edn., 2058 A.D.). The first law is that a robot may not injure a human, or through inaction allow a human to come to harm. Second, orders given by humans must be obeyed, unless that would conflict with the first law. Third, robots must protect their own existence, unless that conflicts with the first or second laws.

A blanket rule not to harm humans is obviously inadequate when forced to choose between the lesser of two evils. Asimov himself later added a "zeroth" law, which said that a robot's highest duty was to humanity as a whole. In one of his last novels, a robot is asked how it could ever determine what is injurious to humanity as a whole. "Precisely, sir," the robot replies. "In theory, the Zeroth Law was the answer to our problems. In practice, we could never decide."

QUESTION 3.1: TROLLEYOLOGY
DEGREE OF DIFFICULTY: MEDIUM

Imagine that you are designing the program that will determine how a self-driving car will behave in an accident. Its first priority would be to avoid a collision entirely; if that is not possible, the car can still make relevant choices. Hitting the fewest pedestrians would be an obvious priority, but what if the car determines that the only way to avoid killing a group of schoolchildren is to drive itself (and the driver) off a cliff? What should the car be programmed to do: kill the schoolchildren or kill the driver?

Answer on page 97.

3.2 NEWCOMB'S PARADOX

An indication that a problem amounts to a conundrum is that rational people reach entirely different conclusions as to the proper answer. First devised in 1960 by a professor at the University of California, Newcomb's Paradox is one of the best examples of this.

Imagine playing a game with a supercomputer that is said to possess the power of prediction. You are presented with two boxes: the first is opaque; the second is transparent and holds a thousand dollars. You are then asked whether you will take the contents of both boxes, or only the first box.

The catch is that the machine claims to know what you are going to do — indeed, in hundreds of games with other players, it has never been wrong. And so, before you make your choice, the computer predicts whether you will take both boxes, or just the opaque one. If it predicts that you will take *both* boxes, the first box is left empty. But if the computer predicts that you will take only the *first* box, then it places a million dollars inside. So what do you choose?[2]

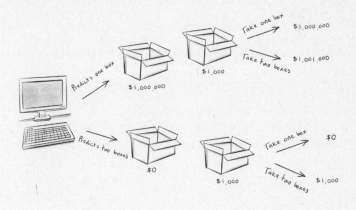

---

2 *Being Arcadia*, chapter 4.

The fact that the boxes contain dollars is arbitrary — it could be jewels or puppies — but it can be assumed that your aim is to get the largest amount that you can. The difficulty is that there are two ways to try to do so.

On the one hand, rationally, it makes sense to choose both boxes. Whichever prediction has been made, that brings you a higher return in each case. If the computer predicted that you would take both boxes, you get a thousand dollars instead of nothing; if it predicted you would take one box, you get a million dollars and an extra thousand.

On the other hand, the supercomputer has never been wrong. If we exclude the possibility of outwitting the machine, then we can rule out the scenarios in which you get either none or all of the money. So the rational choice is only between getting a million dollars or a thousand. In which case you should choose only the first box.

So which is correct? Your guess is as good as mine.

QUESTION 3.2: NEWCOMB'S PARADOX
DEGREE OF DIFFICULTY: HEAD-SCRATCHING

You are presented with two boxes, this time both are opaque. You are told that one has a sum of money in it, and the other has double that amount.

You choose one box, but are not allowed to open it. You are then offered the chance to switch boxes.

Should you switch?

A friend who has studied probability urges you to do so. "Look," she says. "Let's say that the box you have chosen has M dollars in it. If you switch now, there's a 50% chance that the other box has 2M and a 50% chance that it has $\frac{M}{2}$.

"In other words, your expected value is

$$\frac{1}{2}(2M) + \frac{1}{2}\left(\frac{M}{2}\right) = \frac{5}{4}M$$

"That's more than the M in your current box, so your best bet is to switch."

Should you?

Answer on page 97.

3.3 MONTY HALL

The Monty Hall problem has the unusual honour of being named after the host of a TV game show. Based loosely on the show *Let's Make a Deal*, it was posed in a letter to *American Statistician* by Steve Selvin in 1975. Though it is often now described with respect to three doors, the original problem involved three boxes in the manner of the TV game show.

Imagine, then, that there are three boxes: one red, one yellow, and one blue.[3] Inside one of them is a prize — keys to a new car, perhaps. The other two are empty.

You are asked to pick one. When you have done so, the person running the game opens one of the two boxes that you did not select and reveals that it is empty.

Now comes the test: you are offered the chance to switch from the box you selected to the other remaining box. Should you do so?

If you hesitate, you are not alone. Many people either believe that the odds of them having chosen correctly have not changed, or that the removal of a different box actually strengthens their belief that the box they first chose is correct.

Mathematics proves, however, that they are wrong.

When first asked to choose, you had a one in three chance of choosing the correct box. Let us assume you picked the yellow box. In the event that you happened to choose correctly, it would be a mistake to switch. But that is only a one-third chance. If the prize was in fact in the red box, you were wrong. In that situation, the blue box would have been removed and it would be a mistake *not* to switch. Similarly, if the prize was in the blue box, it is the red box that would have been removed

---

3   *Raising Arcadia*, chapter 4.

and again you would have won by switching. So in two of the possible three scenarios, you are better off switching from your original choice.

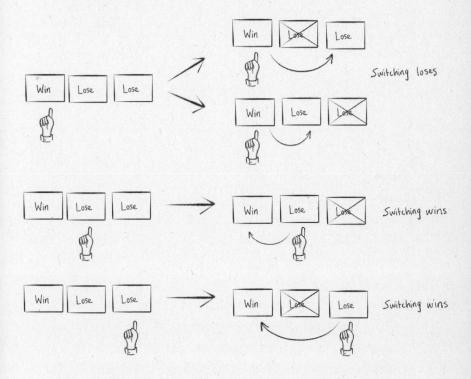

It may be clearer if we imagine not three but three hundred boxes. You choose one, and then two hundred and ninety-eight other boxes are removed, leaving the one you chose and one other. The prize, you are assured, is in one of the two boxes. Now, surely you would switch? (Not everyone would, but probability says that they *should*.)

QUESTION 3.3: MONTY HALL
DEGREE OF DIFFICULTY: HEAD-SCRATCHING

The Monty Hall problem is, for some reason, commonly expressed in terms of three doors. Behind one is a car; behind each of the other two is a goat. (You are, presumably, expected to go for the car.)[4]

In this variation, some of the same principles of probability apply, but you play alone.

Imagine there are three cards, on each of which is a different number. Your aim is to get the highest number. You can turn over one, two, or all three cards. The catch is that you are stuck with the last number you turn over. (Oh, and you do not know how high the numbers go.)

Is there a strategy that will improve your odds above one in three?

Answer on page 98.

---

4   A riddle that echoes this also has three doors: behind one is a blazing inferno, behind another is a master swordsman intent on killing you, behind the third is a lion that has not eaten in three months. Which door do you choose? The one with the lion, of course. It is dead.

3.4 TRUEL

One of the most famous movies set in the American West is entitled "The Good, the Bad, and the Ugly". Starring Clint Eastwood, it ends in a climactic three-way duel in which everyone shoots at everyone else.

The idea of a three-way duel first seems to have appeared in an early nineteenth century novel, but entered into game theory in the 1960s in a more stylised form. At this point, the neologism "truel" was also coined.

Imagine, if you will, that Anna, Bruce, and Candy are three gunslingers in a truel. (Let us not inquire into their goodness, badness, or ugliness.) The rules in this truel are as follows: they take turns to shoot and only get to shoot one bullet each time. They can choose where to aim, but they always have the same chance of hitting their target. Anna hits it one-third of the time, Bruce hits it two-thirds of the time, and dead-eye Candy hits it every single time. Anna gets to shoot first, then Bruce, then Candy, then back to Anna and so on until only one of them is standing.[5]

The question is: what should Anna do?

Logically, we might think that she has a one-third chance of hitting her target, and so needs to decide whether to aim at Bruce or Candy.

For the purposes of this game, a shot either kills or misses completely. If she shoots at Bruce, then she has a one-in-three chance of hitting. That's the good news. The bad news is that it is Candy's shot next and Candy never misses. So one third of the time Anna dies.

---

5 *Finding Arcadia*, chapter 10.

She has a *two*-thirds chance of missing Bruce, though. In that case, Bruce would almost certainly aim at Candy, who is the most dangerous. Two thirds of the time Bruce will hit. Then it's back to Anna and Bruce. Still preferable to being left with Candy.

What if she aims at Candy? A one-third chance of hitting, in which case Bruce gets a free shot back at her. If she misses, Bruce will probably also aim at Candy.

As it is possible that Anna and Bruce might go on missing each other for some time, the maths become a little complicated[6] — but in either scenario, almost three-quarters of the time she would end up dead. The odds are fractionally better if she aims at Candy first.

But is there another option? She has the advantage of firing first — or does she? If she hits a target, it doesn't seem to help. If she hits Bruce, Candy gets her every time. If she hits Candy, Bruce has a free shot at her.

Unless she does something else.

Unless she shoots at … the ground.

The odds of dying are still high, but her chance of survival goes up from just over thirty percent to just under forty percent.

---

6   If the truel lasts more than two rounds, it is because Candy — who never misses — is dead. Assuming Anna aims at Candy, the possibilities of Anna surviving the first round are if (i) Anna hits Candy, then Bruce shoots at Anna and misses; (ii) Anna misses Candy, then Bruce shoots Candy and hits; or (iii) Anna and Bruce both miss Candy, who shoots Bruce. The probabilities of Anna surviving are therefore $\frac{1}{3^2} + \frac{2^2}{3^2} + \frac{2}{3^2} = \frac{7}{9}$. But if she intentionally shoots at the ground, she survives if (iv) Bruce hits Candy or (v) Bruce misses Candy, who shoots Bruce. That probability is $\frac{2}{3} + \frac{1}{3} = 1$. In scenarios where Candy lives, Anna has a $\frac{1}{3}$ chance of survival (she either hits the first time or is shot). In the other scenarios, it leads to a shootout between Anna and Bruce, with Anna shooting first. The chances of Anna winning *that* are $\frac{1}{3} + \frac{2}{3^3} + \frac{2^2}{3^5} + \cdots + \frac{2^n}{3^{(2n+1)}} \approx 0.43$. (Such a shootout could, in theory, go on forever.) So if she shoots at Candy, her chances of survival are $\left(\frac{1}{3^2} + \frac{2^2}{3^2}\right) 0.43 + \frac{2}{3^3} \approx 0.31$ or 31%. If she shoots at the ground, her chances are $\left(\frac{2}{3}\right) 0.43 + \frac{1}{3^2} \approx 0.40$ or 40%.

QUESTION 3.4: TRUEL
DEGREE OF DIFFICULTY: MEDIUM

You are an amateur hunter looking for deer when you stumble upon a tiger. You are downwind and it does not see or smell you, so you decide to follow it for a time. It leads you a short way through the forest away from your vehicle, when a low growl indicates that it senses danger. The hair on its arched back is raised; you follow its line of sight and spot the same grizzly bear that has caused it to freeze. The bear's eyes meet yours and it rears up onto its hind legs. Now the tiger turns and sees you also.

You have only one shell in your shotgun and patchy aim. You generally hit your target only one-third of the time. You know that humans have a poor record fighting tigers. "Don't bother to run", is the advice that you remember — all that will mean is that you will die tired.

As for grizzly bears, you recall that a bear will mainly fight if it sees you as a threat or if you run. If you play dead, you will have a fifty-fifty chance of surviving.

If the tiger and the bear fight, the tiger is more agile and has deadlier claws and teeth — but the bear is far larger and has greater stamina. You estimate that two-thirds of the time the tiger will win.

What should you do?

Answer on page 100.

3.5 A LOT OF HOT AIR

Lateral thinking literally means conceiving of something from the side, generally referring to an approach to problem-solving that is indirect and creative. If, on the face of it, your choice is between A and B and neither seems correct, see if it is possible to introduce other letters of the alphabet. Or perhaps the wrong question is being asked.

Imagine, for example, that you are stranded on a desert island. There is food and water, but no means of communication with the mainland. No mobile phones. It is not clear when — or whether — a rescue ship will come.[7]

You are not alone on this island. In addition to yourself, there are three other people. The first is an old woman whom you have only just met. She is clearly unwell and in need of medical attention; if she does not get to a hospital soon, it is possible that she will die. The second person is an old school friend of yours, whom you have not seen in years. While at school he saved your life—a debt you promised to repay, but have not since had the chance. His wife is in hospital on the mainland, about to give birth to their first child. Lastly, the third person is someone you met only recently, but who you are convinced is the love of your life. All of you want to get off the island. The sun is beginning to set, it starts to rain, and there is no shelter to speak of.

Fortunately, you are an amateur hot air balloonist. You have your balloon in working order, and the prevailing wind will carry you to the mainland and safety by sundown. All you would have to do is take off and land, though you can only go one way.

There is an important constraint: your basket is big enough only to carry one other passenger. And so the question is: do

---

7 *Finding Arcadia*, chapter 2.

you take the dying old woman, your healthy friend, or your new sweetheart?

The logical approach to this is to consider the pros and cons of taking each person. A humanitarian approach might be to take the old woman, who seems to be facing the greatest risk. An approach that privileges moral obligation might see the value in repaying the debt owed to the friend. A more selfish answer might be to take your sweetheart — or to abandon all three and take the balloon yourself.

But there is another approach. Another letter of the alphabet other than A, B, or C.

Assuming that piloting a balloon is not that hard and that you have recently learned it, you could give your old friend a quick course in ballooning and then tell him to take the old woman to the hospital where his wife is about to give birth. You might also ask him to send a rescue party for you and the love of your life, seeking shelter together in the meantime from the rain.

QUESTION 3.5: A LOT OF HOT AIR
DEGREE OF DIFFICULTY: MEDIUM

Some months after being rescued from the desert island, you reunite with the old friend (who made it to his wife's side to welcome their first child), the old woman (who got the medical treatment she needed), and your sweetheart (to whom you are now engaged). You celebrate by taking them up in a hot air balloon on a crystal clear morning, basking in the crisp air as the sun rises majestically above the horizon.

Unfortunately, an unseasonably strong breeze blows you off course. You find yourselves drifting, out of fuel and beginning to lose altitude as you float across farmland and towards a nearby city. You and the old friend (who has also kept up ballooning) quickly see that your current trajectory heads towards high-tension power lines. If you collide with the wires, it will cause the nylon envelope to catch fire; but if you shed some weight, the balloon might fly over them.

The two of you look around the wicker basket in which the four of you now stand, dangling at the mercy of the summer breeze. The useless burner is firmly attached to the basket and you just dropped the last sandbag. The ropes attached to the balloon itself sit in neat coils on the floor. You and your old friend are the heaviest in the basket, but also the strongest. The thought crosses your mind that strength might be a factor if it comes to throwing someone overboard.

What do you do?

Answer on page 100.

CONCLUSION: AS SIMPLE AS POSSIBLE – BUT NO SIMPLER

*Be good – and if you can't be good
be quick and don't get caught.*

*Love always
Moira*

Many of the codes, puzzles, and conundrums in this book required you to think laterally or to simplify a question in order to find an answer. We conclude with some bonus questions where there are two ways to solve them. In each case, a long and painstaking method will get you the result — in some cases requiring elaborate mathematical operations. But for each question there is also a faster, simpler method that will get you the answer.

Take, for example, a problem in which two cars are 90 kilometres apart on a single lane road. They start driving towards each other at 45 kilometres per hour. At the exact moment that they start driving, a bug leaves the bonnet of one car and, moving at exactly twice that speed, flies towards the other car. When it reaches the second car, it instantly turns around and flies back towards the first car. By that stage, the first car is getting closer to the second, but the insect immediately turns once more and flies backwards and forwards between the two cars, until finally it is squashed when the two cars collide at the midpoint of the road. The question is: how far did the bug travel before its untimely demise?

Now, one method is to total up the distance that it covered. As it is flying twice as fast as the cars, it will reach the second car for the first time when the cars have covered 30km and the bug has covered 60km.

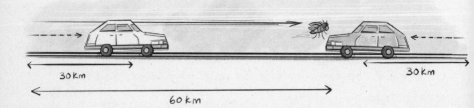

So far, so good. It instantly turns around and flies back. As the bug moves twice as fast as the cars, the next point at which it turns is after the cars have completed one-third of the distance. So, the second turn is after one-third of the remaining 30km, or 10 km, with the fly having covered twice that distance, or 20km.

The cars are now 10 km apart. The third turn would therefore be after the cars have travelled a further $3\frac{1}{3}$km, while the fly has travelled $6\frac{2}{3}$km.

This is clearly starting to get complicated. You may have worked out that the each time the fly traverses one-third of the previous distance: 60km, 20km, $6\frac{2}{3}$km. You can keep summing these amounts, so the next distance would be $2\frac{2}{9}$km, then $\frac{20}{27}$ km and so on with an ever-diminishing distance.

The distance is therefore the sum of an infinite series of numbers, which can be represented as an endless sum:

$$x = 90\left(\frac{2}{3} + \frac{2}{3^2} + \frac{2}{3^3} + \frac{2}{3^4} + \cdots\right)$$

Or by the equation:

$$x = 90\sum_{n=1}^{\infty}\frac{2}{3^n}$$

But don't panic! There is a much simpler way to solve this question. We need to work out the distance that the fly travels, but we already know its speed. An alternative to measuring each leg of its journey is to work out the duration of its flight.

Go back to the start of the problem. Two cars head towards each other at 45km/h. How far do they travel? Half of 90km is 45km. So for how long do they drive before smashing? One hour.

We know that the fly gets squashed when they crash, so it has also been flying for an hour. We know its speed is 90km/h, so it has flown … 90km.

(Yes, that is what the fancy equations equal also.)

So good luck with the final questions. And if you find yourself doing elaborate mathematical steps, then pause — and see if there is a shortcut that you missed.

QUESTION 4.1: BABY BLUES
DEGREE OF DIFFICULTY: MEDIUM

Imagine a town in which every family wants to have a baby girl. There are no restrictions on the number of births, so any family that has a boy can keep on having children until they have a girl — and they do. Once a family does have a baby girl, however, they stop having children entirely. So one family might have a girl and that is their only child. Another family has a boy, then another boy, then another boy, then a girl, and stops. It is forbidden to check the sex of a child before birth and so the possibility of abortion can be ignored.

This practice has been going on for centuries and, surprisingly, all the births are single births — no twins, triplets, and so on. What is the proportion of girls to boys born in this town?

Answer on page 101.

QUESTION 4.2: DEATH BY ALGEBRA
DEGREE OF DIFFICULTY: MEDIUM

If we have an equation $(x+a)(x-b)$ it can be expanded to $x^2-bx+ax-ab$.

If we have an equation $(x+a)(x-b)(x+c)$ it can be expanded to $x^3+cx^2-bx^2-bcx+ax^2+acx-abx-abc$.

Now, expand the following equation:

$(x+a)(x-b)(x+c)(x-d)(x+e) ... (x-z)$

Answer on page 103.

QUESTION 4.3: THE FINAL PROBLEM
DEGREE OF DIFFICULTY: EASY

You have gone on a boat trip with five other people, each wearing a different coloured hat and shirt. The trip goes horribly wrong.

Gerald's hat was red and his murderer's hat was not black. The person wearing the yellow hat and red shirt was killed by someone whose hat and shirt were the same colour. Janine wore a yellow shirt and died at the hands of someone whose shirt was not the colour of her own hat. David had a green hat; when he was slain, he was wearing a shirt the same colour as Betty's hat when she was killed.

When police board the boat, they learn all this information and soon make an arrest. How did they identify the murderer?

Answer on page 103.

ANSWERS

PART 1

1.1 CIPHERS

The following key should enable you to read the message.

♋	♌	♍	♎	♏	♐	♑
A	B	C	D	E	F	G

♒	♓	*et*	&	●	○	■
H	I	J	K	L	M	N

☐	▣	❏	❐	◆	◆	◆
O	P	Q	R	S	T	U

❖	☠	⊠	⊡	⌘
V	W	X	Y	Z

1.2 HIDDEN IN PLAIN SIGHT

Look at the first letter of each seventh word. Then think what "L" might refer to. Then use a ruler or look carefully at the text.

PART 2

2.1 MATCHSTICKS

To remove the fly from the wineglass, take one match from the side of the glass and place it parallel with the stem below, then slide the bottom of the glass across:

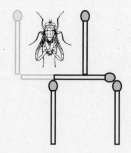

For the three square question, take two matches from the top left and start a new square at the lower right side of the shape. Then move the match from the right hand side of the bottom of the original shape to complete that square.

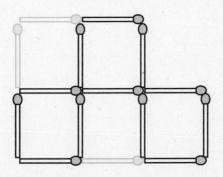

2.2 WATER, WATER, EVERYWHERE

Once again, the solution requires you to treat the jugs not only as containers of water when they are full, but having space for additional water when they are not.

First, fill the five-litre jug with water from the eight-litre jug; then, fill the three-litre jug with the water you just put in the five-litre jug — but don't spill any! Now the eight-litre jug has three litres left in it, the five-litre jug has two litres in it, and the three-litre jug is full.

Pour those last three litres *back* into the eight-litre jug, which now has six litres in it. Tip the remaining two litres from the five-litre jug into the empty three-litre jug. Pour five litres from the eight-litre jug into the five-litre jug, and then use *that* to top up the three litre jug until it is full. Now the eight-litre jug has one litre in it, the five litre jug has four litres, and the three litre jug is full.

Tip the three-litre jug's contents back into the first jug and you have four litres in each of the two larger jugs. (It is probably clear why a puzzle of this nature did not feature in the *Raising Arcadia* trilogy.)

2.3 CRY ME A RIVER

Unlike the wolf-goat-cabbage problem, you could start this problem in different ways. The fastest solution begins with one missionary and one cannibal crossing together. The missionary returns the raft to the original riverbank.

Next two cannibals go over together, with one of them returning. There are now three missionaries and one cannibal at the starting point, with two cannibals on the other side.

Two missionaries now go over together, and one missionary and one cannibal return. Now we have two missionaries and two cannibals where they started, and one of each where they want to go.

Both the remaining missionaries board the raft to the other side and send the cannibal back. She picks up one of the two cannibals, delivers him to the destination, then returns to pick up the last cannibal.

Simple! (But, once again, an argument for a bigger boat or, perhaps, some handcuffs for the cannibals.)

2.4 TO CHANGE A LIGHTBULB

It is possible — but somewhat laborious — to answer this by tracking what actually happens. Person 1 switches them all on, person 2 switches every second light off, person 3 switches the third light off but the sixth light goes back on, and so forth. You can represent this in a table:

Bulb	Status after person number (O=on, X=off)								
	1	2	3	4	5	6	7	8	9
1st	O	O	O	O	O	O	O	O	O
2nd	O	X	X	X	X	X	X	X	X
3rd	O	O	X	X	X	X	X	X	X
4th	O	X	X	O	O	O	O	O	O
5th	O	O	O	O	X	X	X	X	X
6th	O	X	O	O	O	X	X	X	X
7th	O	O	O	O	O	O	X	X	X
8th	O	X	X	O	O	O	O	X	X
9th	O	O	X	X	X	X	X	X	O

But to do this up to one hundred would be fairly tiresome. You may be able to see a pattern already: after nine people have walked the corridor, the first nine lightbulbs will remain in their current status: numbers 1, 4, and 9 on, the rest are off.

What is special about these numbers? They are squares. That is, one is equal to one times one; four is equal to two times two; nine is equal to three times three. That is important because what is really happening here is that every light is being switched on and off in accordance with its factors: the numbers that evenly divide it. Factors come in pairs. So if you pick a number — say, 52 — the numbers that evenly divide it are 1x52, 2x26, and 4x13.

In other words, the people who will tug on the 52nd lightbulb are persons number 1, 2, 4, 13, 26, and 52. As every second tug switches the light off, we know that the 52nd bulb is off. This would be true for most numbers, but squares have an odd number of factors. Thus the numbers that evenly divide 64, say, are 1x64, 2x32, 4x16, and 8x8. Hence the factors are 1, 2, 4, 8,

16, 32, and 64. Because this is an odd number, we know that the light would be left on.

So the answer to the question is that all the square numbers would be on: 1, 4, 9, 16, 25, 36, 49, 64, 81, 100 — 10 lightbulbs.

2.5 MURDER BY NUMBERS

(a) The next number in the sequence is "100" — the next number that does not include the letter "t".

(b) The next is "TH". The hint was that this is in a section on numbers and the sequence is 1st, 2nd, 3rd, 4th, and so 5th.

(c) The next number is "5". On this occasion, each number is the number of letters in the previous number. So "one million six hundred thousand" has 28 letters, "twenty-eight" has 11 letters, "eleven" has 6 letters, "six" has 3 letters, and "three" has 5 letters.

2.6 CHESS

This is a somewhat devious puzzle. It is tempting to promote the pawn to queen, but it will be taken by the king. There are various ways to reach checkmate, though they each take at least four moves.[1]

It is possible, however, to mate in one, though it depends on an older reading of the rules of chess. Note the hints that this is a nineteenth century puzzle and that the rules of chess then allowed promotion of a pawn to *any* other piece. If you want to try again, stop reading now and go back to the puzzle.

Still scratching your head? The solution is to promote the white pawn to a *black knight*. It might sound crazy to transform one of your pieces into one of your opponent's, but in this rare case, it wins the game by revealing check from the rook and effectively blocking black's only path of escape.

---

1   For example: (1) Kb5 Kb8 (2) Kc6 Ka7 (3) b8=R+ Kxb8 (4) Rb7#.

Note that this move would be illegal today, as the World Chess Federation's rules of chess now state that a pawn reaching the furthest rank must be promoted to "a queen, rook, bishop or knight *of the same colour*".

2.7 WHICH WIRE?

This is a variation on a classic puzzle commonly set on an island in which some of the inhabitants always tell the truth and some always lie. The problem is that in asking one question that has a yes/no answer, you do not know whether it is true or false. So if you ask one of the twins: "Should I cut the purple wire?" If she says "Yes", you do not know whether she is telling the truth or not.

The solution is to get more information out of one question so that it does not matter whether you ask the truth-teller or the liar. Drawing on the fact that you know that they consistently lie and tell the truth, you can do this by asking one of them (it does not matter which): "If I asked your twin whether the purple wire disarms the bomb, would she say that it does?"

If the twin you are asking speaks the truth, she knows that her sister always lies and so whatever answer she gives you will be the incorrect one. If the twin you ask is the liar, she knows that her sister would tell you the truth, but she will tell you the opposite. So you know that whatever answer you get to your question is wrong. Thus, if you are told "yes", you should cut the brown wire, while if you are told "no", you should go ahead and cut the purple wire anyway.

2.8 FIRE!

If you thought you could chop a quarter off one of the pieces of string, you have not read the question.

Measuring time is difficult because the only certain period is four minutes for an entire length of string. That is longer than the three minutes that we need — unless you start a second fire. If you light one of the pieces of string at both ends, it will now burn out in two minutes. At the same time that you light both ends of the first string, light one end of the second. Now when the two flames on the first string meet, light the other end of the second string. It would have continued burning for two minutes, but now that it is burning at both ends, it will be consumed in one minute — giving you the 2 + 1 = 3 minutes that you need.

2.9 WALK A MILE IN SOMEONE ELSE'S HAT

The crowns were either gold or silver. If two of the students had been wearing silver crowns, they would not all have raised their hands to show that they could see a gold crown. So there is at most one silver crown.

Yet if any of them could see one silver crown and one gold crown, he or she would know immediately that his or her own crown must be gold. The fact that none of them guesses immediately means that this is not the case, and therefore none of them is wearing a silver crown.

Hence the only possibility is that they are all wearing gold crowns — apart from Albert, who remains in his barrel.

2.10 IMPOSSIBLE PUZZLES

As in the previous example, the solution is reached by eliminating every impossible answer. We start with ten possibilities:

May 15, May 16, May 19
June 17, June 18
July 14, July 16
August 14, August 15, August 17

Albert, who knows the month, says that he knows that Bernard cannot know the answer. Bernard, who knows the day, would only know the answer if the day was unique: if it was 18, he would know her birthday was June 18; if it was 19, he would know the answer was May 19. For Albert to be certain that Bernard does *not* know, he must be able to rule out those months completely.

So we are left with:

July 14, July 16
August 14, August 15, August 17

Now Bernard states that he knows. He would have deduced the same thing as Albert, meaning he now knows that the month is July or August. He knows the day, and so for him to have the answer now rules out the possibility that it was 14, as he would not have known whether that pointed to July 14 or August 14.

The remaining possible answers are therefore:

July 16
August 15, August 17

At this point, Albert also says that he knows when her birthday is. Since he knows the month, it must be that the remaining possible answer has only one option in that month, meaning that Cheryl's birthday is July 16.

As one might expect, many commentators on social media who gave up on the puzzle itself took to questioning Cheryl's motivation for introducing herself to these new friends in such an odd — dare one say puzzling — way.

2.11 LOGICAL PIRATES

A useful approach to a puzzle that is moderately complex is to try to simplify it. Rather than seven pirates, how would we solve the puzzle if there were only two pirates?

That would be simple: the senior pirate would keep all 100 coins to himself. He would vote in favour, the other pirate would vote against, but half the votes is sufficient: the pirate gets all the gold.

What if there were three pirates? Now the most senior knows that if he goes overboard, it will be down to two pirates. In that scenario, the junior pirate gets nothing. So to win his support, a single gold coin would suffice. So now the most senior pirate gets 99 coins, the second gets nothing, while the third gets one coin. (Hopefully not counterfeit.)

Recall that all the pirates are logical, so they have also each worked this out. With four pirates, the most senior knows that he needs to bribe the pirate who would get nothing if there were three pirates left, so he gives one coin to the third most senior pirate (the one who would be second most senior if there were only three pirates) and, once again, gets to keep 99 coins.

With five pirates, the most senior pirate needs two other pirates to support him. By bribing the two pirates who get nothing in the scenario where there are four pirates, he keeps 98 coins while the other two get one each.

For six pirates, again two votes are required and this can be secured by bribing the two pirates who lost out in the five-pirate scenario.

And so, we arrive at seven pirates. By now, it should be clear that all one needs to do is win the support of three pirates, those being the three who would get nothing if you were thrown overboard. So you bribe the third, fifth, and seventh most senior pirates with one coin each and keep 97 coins to yourself.

Arr!

PART 3

3.1 TROLLEYOLOGY

Really? You really thought there was an "answer" to this?

Executives at Mercedes-Benz are on record saying that they would prioritise the lives of passengers of its cars over those of any pedestrians. This, perhaps, reflects another approach in addition to the utilitarianism and deontology mentioned earlier: commercialism.

A paper recently published in *Science* backs this up with survey findings: while many people approve of such cars sacrificing their passengers to save other people in theory, they are unlikely to buy or ride in a car programmed in that way in practice.[2]

3.2 NEWCOMB'S PARADOX

Your friend is mistaken. If what she concluded were true, then you might equally decide not to open the second box, but denote

---

2   Jean-François Bonnefon, Azim Shariff & Iyad Rahwan, "The Social Dilemma of Autonomous Vehicles" (2016) *Science*, Vol. 352(6293), p. 1573.

its value as N. If you went through the same process, you would conclude that it makes sense to switch again for an expected value of $\frac{5}{4} N$, and then to continue switching forever.

The problem is that the value of M is not fixed within the problem. If we assign values to the boxes this can be made clearer. Let us say that one box contains $10 and the other box contains $20.

There is a 50% chance that you chose the $10 box, and an equal chance that you chose the $20 box. If you switch, you therefore have an equal chance of gaining money and losing it. Either way, your true expected value is:

$$\tfrac{1}{2}(\$10) + \tfrac{1}{2}(-\$10) = 0$$

3.3 MONTY HALL

You do not have a helpful host to remove one of the cards (or a goat to eat one), but it is possible to improve your odds from one in three to one in two. As in the Monty Hall problem, it may help to think in terms of possible choices and the probability behind them.

There is a one in three chance that you pick the highest card first. But if you do nothing more than that, your chance of being correct stays at one in three.

Turning over a second card gives us more information and that is the key to improving our odds. If it is higher than the first card, that gives us some information; if it is lower, that also gives us information.

As mentioned, there is a one in three chance that we were right the first time. Discarding that card means a one-third chance we lose. But if the next card is higher, then either we first picked the lowest card and this is the middle or the highest card, or else we picked the middle card and this is definitely the highest card. So if the second card is higher, we should hang onto it.

If the second card is lower, then either we picked the highest card first, in which case all is lost, or else we picked the middle card first and this is the lowest card. Either way, there is no harm and a chance that we get a higher card by now taking a third card.

As the diagram below shows, the result is that of six equally likely outcomes, turning over a second card and stopping if it is higher than the first gives you an even chance of winning.

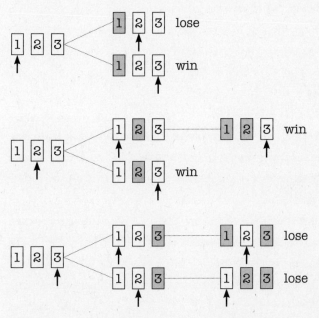

(Martin Garnder posed a more complicated version of this problem in *Scientific American* in 1960. It is sometimes known as the "Secretary Problem" and involves the mathematical theory of optimal stopping.)

3.4 TRUEL

If you were running through probability scenarios based on shooting the tiger or the bear, you probably deserve to be eaten. This is not a truel and it is unlikely that either animal *wants* to attack you.

Remember that you have a gun and that you have a vehicle. So back slowly away towards that vehicle. If either animal looks like it is going to charge you, shoot the shotgun in the general direction of both beasts. Hopefully you will not injure either of the creatures — who were, after all, just minding their own business when you came in search of a defenceless deer that you wanted to murder for some reason — but you may succeed in scaring them away just long enough for you to reach the car.

(Please do not try this in real life.)

3.5 A LOT OF HOT AIR

What goes up, must come down. To delay that eventuality, lightening the load might indeed enable the balloon to ascend over the power lines. One possibility is, therefore, to throw someone overboard — but whom? This is a staple of the balloon debates used at schools around the world. Should Albert Einstein or Mother Teresa be hurled out of the basket? What if the choice is between a middle-aged man who has spent his life helping the community, or a young woman who has yet to have a chance to serve hers?

But in this case, even if you were to clear the power lines, you are headed towards a city and would eventually have to land. Throwing one person overboard, or even two, would merely postpone the inevitable.

Rather than keep on going up, however, the alternative is to come down immediately. Hot air balloons are controlled not only by the burners that heat the air inside them, but also by the vents that allow that hot air to escape. Most have a parachute vent or other mechanism to allow it to descend quickly.

The farmland over which you are floating may well run the risk of a rough landing or an encounter with cattle, but that is preferable to an uncertain chance of clearing the power lines — and the inevitable homicide charge that would follow your landing afterwards.

CONCLUSION

4.1 BABY BLUES

There is, as you may have guessed, more than one way to answer this question.

It is possible to do so by using probability. For the first child in any family, there is a 50 percent chance that it is a girl.[3] If the number 1 represents certainty, this is a probability of 0.5. Such a family has no more children. There is an equal chance that it is a boy, after which the family would have another child. The chances of having two boys in a row would be 0.5 x 0.5 or 0.25. The chances of having a boy and then a girl are the same.

So regardless of how many people there are in this town, we could add up the probabilities to work out the total proportion of girls:

---

3 OK, so it is not *exactly* equal. See Steven Hecht Orzack et al., "The Human Sex Ratio from Conception to Birth" (2015) *Proceedings of the National Academy of Sciences*, Vol. 112(16), p. E2102. Note also that the question asks about the number of babies born, so differences in life expectancy can be disregarded.

Birth order	Probability	Number of girls and boys
G	0.5	G=1, B=0
BG	0.25	G=1, B=1
BBG	0.125	G=1, B=2
BBBG	0.0625	G=1, B=3

And so on, theoretically, to an infinite (or at least very large) number of boys followed by a girl.

In each of these scenarios, every family has exactly one girl. So how many boys do they have? There's a 0.5 chance that they had zero, a 0.25 chance they had one, a 0.125 chance they had two, a 0.0625 chance they had three and so on. This can be represented by the endless sum:

$$X = \frac{1}{2^2} + \frac{2}{2^3} + \frac{3}{2^4} + \cdots + \frac{n}{2^{(n+1)}}$$

Or by the equation:

$$X = \sum_{n=1}^{\infty} \frac{n}{2^{(n+1)}}$$

Once again, don't panic! There is an easier way. As the problem states that there is no sex selection involved, for each birth there is a 50-50 chance of a girl or a boy. The fact that a given family stops having children after a girl is born does not alter that probability. So for any number of children you would therefore expect the number of girls and boys to be equal, or in a ratio of 1:1. (And yes, that's what the scary equation also equals: 1.)

4.2 DEATH BY ALGEBRA

You *could* begin expanding the equation, but that would quickly become very complicated. If we start with the first two pairs of brackets:

$$(x+a)(x-b)(x+c) \ldots (x-z) = (x^2-bx+ax-ab)(x+c) \ldots (x-z)$$

Going to the next bracket gives us:

$$(x+a)(x-b)(x+c) \ldots (x-z) = (x^3+cx^2-bx^2-bcx+ax^2+ acx-abx-abc)(x+d) \ldots (x-z)$$

And eventually we would end up with a very long formula that starts with x^{26} and has around 67 million terms.

As you might have guessed, there is a simpler method. Going through the pairs we can see that the third last one will be ... $(x-x)$. Now, anything multiplied by zero is zero, so the expanded equation, all 67 million terms of it, will equal?

Zero.

4.3 THE FINAL PROBLEM

There were six people on the boat. Five of them are now dead. (Note that the person wearing the yellow hat and red shirt is not Gerald, Janine, David, or Betty, and yet is just as dead.)

Since all five were killed, murdered, slain, and so on, it stands to reason that the person responsible for the murders was ... you!

ACKNOWLEDGMENTS

Many of the codes, puzzles, and conundrums in this book draw upon classical problems, the authors of which are lost to history. Others have apocryphal origins or have entered into public discourse to the extent that identifying a single author would be misleading. The following nevertheless attempts to recognise some of those whose work informed or influenced my own, in addition to those already mentioned in the text.

The self-solving chess problem in section 2.6 is commonly attributed to V. Ropke in a 1942 edition of the Danish chess periodical, *Skakbladet*. The puzzle posed in the same section is of uncertain origin, but I learned of it through the Hebden Bridge Chess Club's website and a 2011 posting.

The history of hat problems similar to those discussed in section 2.9 can be found in an article by Christopher Hardin and Alan Taylor, "An Introduction to Infinite Hat Problems", *Mathematical Intelligencer* (2008) Vol. 30(4), pp. 20–25.

"Cheryl's Birthday" problem, used in section 2.10, was adapted into its current form by Dr. Joseph Yeo Boon Wooi at Singapore's National Institute of Education. Having "gone viral", the problem now has its own Wikipedia page and continues to inspire spirited debate. He offered a "part 2" in the May 2015 issue of Nanyang Technological University's *Hey* magazine. Albert and Bernard now want to know how old Cheryl is:

Cheryl: I have two younger brothers. The product of all our ages (i.e. my age and the ages of my two brothers) is 144, assuming that we use whole numbers for our ages.

Albert: We still don't know your age. What other hints can you give us?

Cheryl: The sum of all our ages is the bus number of this bus that we are on.

Bernard: Of course we know the bus number, but we still don't know your age.

Cheryl: Oh, I forgot to tell you that my brothers have the same age.

Albert and Bernard: Oh, now we know your age.

The answer can be found in this footnote.[1]

A version of the pirate gold puzzle in section 2.11 was, in fact used at one time as part of Oxford University's interviews for computer science. It is now included (with answer) on the "sample interview questions" page of the Oxford admissions website.

There is a vast literature on the trolley problems in section 3.1. Two recent examples are David Edmonds, *Would You Kill the Fat Man? The Trolley Problem and What Your Answer Tells Us*

---

1   The factors of 144 are $2^4 * 3^2$. The only sets of three that multiply to 144 and yet also yield the same sum are: (i) $3 + 6 + 8 = 17$; (ii) $4 + 4 + 9 = 17$; (iii) $2 + 8 + 9 = 19$; (iv) $3 + 4 + 12 = 19$. When they are given the information that the brothers are the same age, it is clear that only (ii) satisfies the constraints and so Cheryl's age is 9.

About Right and Wrong (Princeton: Princeton University Press, 2013) and Thomas Cathcart, *The Trolley Problem; or, Would You Throw the Fat Guy Off the Bridge? A Philosophical Conundrum* (New York: Workman Publishing, 2013). The Moral Machine created by MIT enables you to game out various scenarios and pose your own. It is available at moralmachine.mit.edu.

Steve Selvin's original letter posing the Monty Hall problem used in section 3.3 can be found in *The American Statistician* (1975) Vol. 29(1), p. 67. Precursors include the box paradox in Joseph Bertrand's 1889 book, *Calcul des probabilités* and the three prisoners problem posed by Martin Gardner in a 1959 issue of *Scientific American*.

For a history of the "truel" problem in section 3.4, see D. Marc Kilgour and Stephen J. Brams, "The Truel", *Mathematics Magazine* (1997) Vol. 70(5), pp. 315–326.

A similar problem to the hot air balloon conundrum in section 3.5 is posed in the movie *16 Blocks*, starring Bruce Willis, though the setting is a bus stop on a deserted road and a two-passenger car, rather than a desert island and a hot air balloon.

More general inspiration came from reading Martin Gardner's popular science books and Lewis Carroll's *Symbolic Logic* as a teenager, and listening to the weekly puzzler on NPR's *Car Talk* with Tom and Ray Magliozzi. They retired in 2012, but their show lives on in endless "best of" compilations and the website cartalk.com.

The problems presented in this book have been tested on family and friends, as well as on social media "friends". My thanks to all for their good humour and, especially, for their patience. Errors of logic or style are, of course, the author's alone.

If you enjoyed this book, read the trilogy!

RAISING ARCADIA

Arcadia Greentree knows she isn't exactly normal. But then she discovers she isn't Arcadia Greentree either.

Arcadia sees the world like no one else. Exceptionally observant, the sixteen-year-old is aware of her surroundings in a way that sometimes gets her into trouble—and then out of it again. But then she discovers something odd going on at school, and a tragedy at home forces her to use her skills to catch a killer.

The stunning sequel to Raising Arcadia:

FINDING ARCADIA

To understand the present, Arcadia Greentree must dig into her past.

Her family torn apart by tragedy, Arcadia tries to locate the "professor" whom she believes to be ultimately responsible. A series of clues lead her to Oxford University and a confrontation with her enemy—but all is not as it seems.

The shocking conclusion to the trilogy:

BEING ARCADIA

Arcadia Greentree confronts her past—and her future.

The pieces of Arcadia's life are slowly falling into place when Moira returns to scatter them once more. Arcadia must now choose whether to trust her nemesis as they reveal the dark secret of their birth.

ABOUT THE AUTHOR

 SIMON CHESTERMAN is a Professor and Dean of the National University of Singapore Faculty of Law. Educated in Melbourne, Beijing, and Oxford, he has lived and worked for the past decade in Singapore. He is the author or editor of twenty books, including *One Nation Under Surveillance, Just War or Just Peace?* and *You, The People*. The *Raising Arcadia* trilogy is his first work of fiction.